A DECADE OF
CHAMPIONS

A DECADE OF
CHAMPIONS

SUPER BOWLS XV-XXIV

Nate Aaseng

Lerner Publications Company ■ Minneapolis, Minnesota

ACKNOWLEDGMENTS

Photographs are reproduced through the courtesy of: Vernon J. Biever, pp. 1, 2, 18, 33, 34, 38, 41, 43, 44, 47, 48, 56; San Francisco 49ers, pp. 6, 30, 32, 40, 45; Washington Redskins, pp. 10, 11, 13, 14, 15; James Biever, p. 17; Los Angeles Raiders, pp. 22, 24, 27; Los Angeles Raiders/Russ Reed, p. 20; Los Angeles Raiders/Dan Honda, p. 21; Los Angeles Raiders/Greg Cava, pp. 23, 25, 28; Miami Dolphins, p. 37; New England Patriots/Thomas J. Croke, pp. 50, 54; Chicago Bears, pp. 52 (both), 55; Jerry Pinkus, pp. 58, 60, 63, 64.

Front cover photo by Vernon J. Biever.

Page 1: Del Rodgers, a backup running back for the San Francisco 49ers, is jubilant during a television interview immediately after Super Bowl XXIII.

Page 2: A balloon release at Joe Robbie Stadium set the tone for Super Bowl XXIII.

LIBRARY OF CONGRESS CATALOGING-IN-PUBLICATION DATA
Aaseng, Nathan.
  A decade of champions : Super Bowls XV to XXIV / Nathan Aaseng.
      p. cm.
  Summary: Discusses the Super Bowl winners of the 1980s—the Redskins, the Raiders, the Bears, the Giants, and the 49ers—analyzing how these teams got to the top.
  ISBN 0-8225-1504-0
  1. Super Bowl Game (Football)—History—Juvenile literature.
[1. Super Bowl Game (Football)—History. 2. Football—History.]
I. Title.
GV956.2.S8A17   1991
796.332'648—dc20   90-38607
                                                        CIP
                                                        AC

Manufactured in the United States of America

1 2 3 4 5 6 7 8 9 10 00 99 98 97 96 95 94 93 92 91

Contents

The player of the decade, quarterback Joe Montana, led the San Francisco 49ers to four Super Bowl victories. Montana never seemed to have a bad game in the Super Bowl, winning the MVP award in three of his four appearances.

Introduction

The 1980s turned professional football upside down. The decade was a time for kings to become beggars and for beggars to become kings.

The decade began with a team from the American Football Conference (AFC) dominating a team from the National Football Conference (NFC) in the Super Bowl for the eighth time in nine years. It ended with the NFC champ pummeling the AFC representative for the eighth time in nine years!

The '80s began with the Steelers, Raiders, Dolphins, and Cowboys extending their long reigns of terror over their division rivals. By the time the decade ended, all those teams were struggling for respect. The Raiders, Dolphins, and Cowboys were shut out of the play-offs the last three years of the 1980s, and the Steelers missed the play-offs in two of those three years.

When the '80s began, the San Francisco 49ers were the laughingstock of the league. The decade ended with the red and gold banner of the 49ers flying atop the league. With four Super Bowl victories in a span of nine years, San Francisco dominated the sport as thoroughly in the '80s as the Steelers had in the '70s.

One thing that the '80s shakeup did not change was the curse of the Super Bowl. Every year millions of people sat down to enjoy the biggest single sporting event in the United States, only to be disappointed by the lack of competition. Most Super Bowls offered little that was either entertaining or sporting. From Super Bowl XVII to XXIV, the average margin of victory for the winning team was more than 24 points! Only 3 of the 10 Super Bowls in the decade offered any suspense.

In every year, the champions stormed through the play-offs with such fury that it was difficult to imagine how any team could beat them in the years to come. Each of them, the Bears, the Raiders, the Redskins, the Giants, and especially the 49ers, looked invincible in victory. Sportswriters claimed each Super Bowl champion to be pro football's new dynasty, comparing them to the football powerhouses of the past — the Green Bay Packers of the 1960s, the Miami Dolphins of the early 1970s, and the Pittsburgh Steelers of the late 1970s.

Yet only the 49ers, at the end of the decade, were able to come back after winning one Super Bowl and win another the following year. Nearly every season, a new, almost unbeatable team emerged to trample the reigning champion.

Except for the shift in power from the AFC to the NFC, there seemed to be no pattern to the development of these one-year wonders. None offered a sure-fire formula for success. The Redskins assembled a team of free-agent giants who could win the grimy shoving matches in the trenches. The Raiders channeled the manic energy of some of football's less desirable players into an intimidating lineup. Chicago and New York loaded up their defenses with top draft choices and dared opponents to try to score. With the meticulous attention characteristic of a Rolls-Royce assembly plant, the San Francisco 49ers polished and assembled players to fit an intricate offensive system. Of course, the fact that the 49ers had the player of the decade, Joe Montana, to run the plays didn't hurt the team's chances of winning.

As the '80s drew to a close, the NFC was firmly established as the superior conference, and the 49ers were clearly the class of the league.

CHAPTER 1

Washington Redskins

Super Bowl XVII
Super Bowl XXII

"The future is now," said Washington Redskins management during the 1970s. Impatient with the usual slow rebuilding efforts, the Redskins tried to speed the process by trading batches of future draft choices in exchange for skilled veterans who might help the team immediately.

The "buy now, pay later" scheme did not work. The veterans did not help Washington win a Super Bowl. As those players began to retire, the Redskins were unable to replace them in the lineup because the team had squandered its top draft choices. From 1969 until 1980, Washington had no first-round draft choices. Instead, Redskins officials watched other teams draft the best college players in the first round, while they waited for their picks in the later rounds.

When the team stumbled to a losing mark in 1980, the Redskins appeared doomed to a decade of failure. Because of their impatience, the Redskins had

few highly regarded young players to build a team around. Under normal conditions, the team would have to wait years to get good young athletes and then spend several more years developing them.

Incredibly, it took General Manager Bobby Beathard and Head Coach Joe Gibbs just two years to bring the Redskins from ruin to glory. The 1982 Redskins were a collection of bargain-basement athletes that Beathard had scrounged up. The Redskins' only first-round draft choices were second-year wide receiver Art Monk and rookie offensive lineman Mark May. Almost all the rest of the players had been lightly regarded or completely overlooked by pro scouts.

For example, no one thought enough of Joe Jacoby or Jeff Bostic to draft either of them. George Starke had unsuccessful trials with a couple of pro teams. Yet these three became important members of a powerful offensive

Redskins Coach Joe Gibbs

Some of the Redskins' veteran stars had been discarded by their old teams. Quarterback Joe Theismann had been traded to Washington by Miami, and All-Pro defensive back Tony Peters was traded by Cleveland. Huge defensive tackle Dave Butz had signed with Washington as a free agent after playing at St. Louis. Colorful fullback John Riggins, a former New York Jet, had been so disgruntled with his contract that he had sat out a season before agreeing to play for Washington.

Coach Joe Gibbs took this unpromising assortment of players and molded them into a team. In an era when coaches were trying to outsmart each other with their computer-programmed offenses, Gibbs returned the game to its most basic form—a shoving match. The secret to the Redskins' success was simply this: When big people push against smaller people, the small people generally move backward.

At first, Gibbs' strategies seemed to be worthless. In his first season as head coach, 1981, the Redskins lost their first six games. By the end of the season, however, the players had caught on to Gibbs' methods and finished with a respectable 8-8 mark.

By the next season, 300-pound Hogs such as Jacoby and Russ Grimm were ready to throw their weight around. Behind these human wrecking balls, Riggins was a bulldozer. Coach Gibbs

line. Proudly bearing the name of "Hogs," the enormous Redskin blockers excelled at pushing defensive linemen off the line of scrimmage.

Of Washington's top four linebackers, Rich Milot and Monte Coleman were late-round draft choices; Neil Olkewicz and Mel Kaufman were not selected at all. All-Pro special teams stars Mark Moseley and Mike Nelms had not been drafted either. Wide receiver Charlie Brown was a ninth-round choice, and tight end Clint Didier wasn't drafted until the 12th round.

In fullback John Riggins, the Redskins had a durable, powerful running back to lead the team's ground attack.

sent his rugged, 230-pound fullback slamming into the line an average of 22 times per game in 1982. With defenses forced to dig in to stop Riggins and the Hogs, Joe Theismann was left free to enjoy his finest year as a passer. If both Riggins and Theismann became bogged down at the end of a drive, placekicker Mark Moseley came to the rescue. Moseley was named the National Football League's (NFL's) Most Valuable Player for making 20 of his 21 field-goal tries. Although none of the Redskin defenders was voted to any All-Pro teams, they played very well as a team. Washington allowed a league-

low 128 points as the team bullied its way to an 8-1 record in the strike-shortened 1982 season.

The Redskins had improved so rapidly that many fans, looking at the unfamiliar names on the roster, refused to believe that they were really that good. But with Riggins carrying more and more of the load, the Redskins breezed through their first two play-off tests. After pummeling Detroit, 31-7, Washington beat Minnesota, 21-7. Riggins carried the ball 37 times for 185 yards to control the game against the Vikings.

In the NFC championship game

against the Dallas Cowboys, Riggins pounded into a strong defensive line 36 times for 140 tough yards. Even so, it took a big play from the defense to wrap up the title. With Washington ahead by a touchdown in the fourth quarter, Redskin defensive end Dexter Manley tipped a pass to teammate Darryl Grant. Grant loped 10 yards into the end zone to put the game out of reach, 31-17.

Washington was matched against the Miami Dolphins in Super Bowl XVII. The Dolphins' defense had been nicknamed "The Killer Bees," because 6 of the 11 starters had last names beginning with *B*. The Killer Bees had swarmed all over the quarterbacks in the play-offs, intercepting 10 passes in their last two games. Fresh from shutting down the New York Jets, 14-0, in the AFC championship, Miami posed a rugged challenge to the upstart Redskins' team of leftovers.

Coach Gibbs, however, spotted a mismatch in the lineups. Even though Miami had allowed the fewest total yards in the league, they had ranked no better than 24th against the run. Furthermore, Washington's most powerful blocker, 300-pound Joe Jacoby, would be working against the smallest of the Dolphin linemen, Kim Bokamper. When the teams met for the Super Bowl on January 30, 1983, in the Rose Bowl stadium in Pasadena, California, Gibbs intended to take full advantage of the 50-pound weight difference between those two. Washington would open the game with passes and trick plays to loosen up the defense, and then wear them down with sheer size and strength.

In order for that strategy to work, Washington could not allow the Dolphins to jump out to a big lead. When Miami struck for a sudden touchdown early in the first quarter, Washington's game plan was in danger. On second down and 6 from the Miami 24, Jimmy Cefalo caught a routine 20-yard pass from third-year quarterback David Woodley. The wide receiver then eluded the late-arriving Redskin defense and scampered down the sidelines for a touchdown.

The Dolphins kept the pressure on, driving to a first down at the Redskin 37. Washington escaped further damage, however, when defensive end Dexter Manley broke through for a quarterback sack. His tackle of Woodley jarred the ball loose, and Dave Butz recovered for the Redskins at the 46. Washington's slow-starting offense moved just close enough for Mark Moseley to cut the gap to 7-3 with a 31-yard field goal.

One of Washington's strengths over the years had been its special teams, such as its kickoff unit, its punt-return unit, and its field-goal unit. But in the Super Bowl, the special teams' lackluster performances kept digging the

Redskin receiver Alvin Garrett awaits a pass in the end zone, while Miami's Gerald Small tries to prevent the touchdown.

Redskins into holes. Miami's Fulton Walker gave the Dolphins excellent field position by returning the Redskin kickoff 42 yards. After a short drive, Uwe von Schamann kicked a 20-yard field goal to give Miami a 10-3 lead.

Joe Theismann's crisp passes then launched the Redskin offense on its first impressive drive of the day. He capped the march with a 4-yard toss to Alvin Garrett, and the Redskins had finally made up the early deficit. All that effort, however, was erased in another special teams' lapse. Fulton Walker took the kickoff, veered to the right, cut left

and raced 98 yards for a touchdown. Miami went into the locker room at halftime with a 17-10 lead.

Despite the score, Joe Gibbs believed his strategy was working. Washington had run 35 plays, compared to 22 for Miami. At that rate, the Killer Bees were bound to wear out as they tried to fight off their bigger opponents. The Redskins had outplayed Miami in most phases of the game. If the Redskins could just keep Miami from getting big plays, Washington had a good chance of winning.

In the third quarter, the Dolphins almost forced the turnover that could have won the game for them. After a Moseley field goal had cut the Dolphin lead to 17-13, Washington started another drive from their own 18-yard line. Theismann's first pass attempt was tipped up in the air. As the ball fluttered toward the hands of Miami's Kim Bokamper near the Redskins' goal line, Theismann lunged just in time to bat the ball away and deny Miami an almost-certain touchdown.

The Dolphins could do nothing against the Redskin defense in the second half. Woodley did not complete a pass after halftime, and the Dolphins managed only two first downs in the final 30 minutes of the game.

Meanwhile, the Redskins turned the offense over to Riggins and the Hogs. Miami's weary defenders summoned all their strength to halt a Redskin drive that had reached the Miami 43. Instead of punting on fourth down, however, Washington gambled that they could gain the 1 yard they needed for the first down. The punting unit stayed on the sidelines, and the play called for Riggins to plow through behind Jacoby.

As the teams braced for the snap of the ball, tight end Clint Didier went in motion to the right, then turned back and began jogging in the other direction. Miami cornerback Don McNeal, who was shadowing the tight end, slipped when Didier made his turn. As a result, he was a half step out of position when Riggins burst past the first-down markers and the defensive line. The big fullback easily burst through McNeal's attempted tackle and ran 43 yards for the score. A few minutes later, Riggins carried the ball eight times on a time-killing drive that ended in a 6-yard touchdown pass to Charlie Brown. The Redskins won the game, 27-17.

With the exception of the Redskins' kickoff-coverage unit, the entire Washington team had played well. The defense had stuffed the Miami ground attack and had held David Woodley to 4 completions in 17 attempts. The little wide receivers, known as "The Smurfs," had scored two touchdowns. Theismann had completed 15 of 23 passes. The Hogs had blocked well. But it was Riggins who won the Most Valuable Player

Quarterback Joe Theismann ran the plays for Washington in two of the Redskins' three Super Bowl appearances during the 1980s.

Award. His 38 carries and 166 yards, both Super Bowl records, were judged to be the main reason for Washington's surprising Super Bowl title.

Washington's second Super Bowl title came just as unexpectedly as the first. Although the Redskins remained a strong team throughout the 1980s, they began to lose ground to their division rivals, the New York Giants. In 1987, the Chicago Bears, the San Francisco 49ers, and the defending Super Bowl champion Giants were all thought to be better than Washington.

Coincidentally, Washington's second Super Bowl title also came during a strike year. In 1987, NFL teams hired replacement players for the regular players who went on strike. The Redskins might have missed out on the Super Bowl had their strike replacement team not won all three of its games.

Before the season, Washington had again relied on shrewd trades and detailed scouting to replace veterans. When quarterback Theismann retired, 1984 third-round draft choice Jay Schroeder was given the job. Veteran free agent Doug Williams was signed as a backup to Schroeder. When Riggins' retirement left a huge gap in the offensive backfield, Washington traded for New Orleans workhorse George Rogers and signed United States Football League (USFL) star Kelvin Bryant.

USFL wide receiver Gary Clark and former New England Patriot Ricky Sanders joined Art Monk, holder of the single-season record for pass receptions, as targets for Schroeder's passes. Charles Mann, from lightly-regarded University of Nevada-Reno, joined Dave Butz and Dexter Manley on the defensive line. Washington had surprised experts by using its first-round draft pick in 1983 to take unheralded Darrell Green of Texas-Arlington. Green, however, quickly gained a reputation as a top defender.

As usual, Joe Gibbs produced a winning team. Counting the strike replacement games, Washington finished the season at 11-4 to top the NFC's Eastern Division. The offense shifted from a basic ground attack to a wide open passing game: Clark, Monk, and Sanders combined for 12 touchdowns and more than 2,100 yards in catches. Led by Charles Mann, the Redskin defense racked up 53 sacks. Defensive back Barry Wilburn led the team with 9 interceptions.

Despite the team's impressive statistics, Washington did not look to be Super Bowl material. Injuries slowed Schroeder and Rogers. Schroeder completed fewer than half of his passes and was replaced at quarterback by Williams, a talented but inconsistent player. Rogers

Wide receiver Gary Clark was one of the USFL players Washington signed to shore up the team for another Super Bowl run.

gained just over 600 yards, hardly what the Redskins had come to expect from the power fullback position. On defense, lineman Dexter Manley was no longer the terror of quarterbacks that he had been in the past.

Throughout most of the first play-off game, the Redskins struggled. Trailing 14-0 to the favored home team, the Chicago Bears, Washington seemed headed for a season-ending defeat. But Darrell Green's 52-yard punt return sparked a comeback and a 21-17 win. Washington then beat the Minnesota Vikings, 17-10, with help from a couple of splendid goal-line stands. Although they had not played particularly impressively in either play-off game, the Redskins found themselves heading for a Super Bowl showdown in San Diego against the Denver Broncos.

Denver was returning to the Super Bowl for the second straight year, hoping to make up for losses in the team's two previous Super Bowl appearances. The Broncos had earned their third trip to the Super Bowl by beating the Cleveland Browns, 38-33, in a wild finish in the AFC championship.

Since the AFC was considered weaker than the NFC, the AFC champion would normally have been an underdog in the Super Bowl. But the experts pointed to the mismatch in the crucial backfield positions, predicting that Denver would make a good contest of the game. At quarterback, the Broncos featured John Elway, a talented athlete with a strong arm and a reputation for creating big plays out of disastrous situations. Washington could only counter with Doug Williams, who had played little in recent years. His woeful 9-for-26 performance against the Vikings in the NFC championship fueled suspicion that he was not of championship caliber.

Denver's running attack was led by Sammy Winder, the fifth leading active rusher in the AFC. Washington's ground game was forced to rely on an unknown rookie, Timmy Smith. Smith, a fifth-round draft choice from Texas Tech, had gained only 126 yards all season!

As the game got underway on January 31, 1988, Elway struck quickly with a 56-yard scoring pass to Ricky Nattiel. The Broncos increased their lead to 10-0 with a 24-yard field goal by Rich Karlis. Before the first quarter was over, Washington's Doug Williams was sacked. He fell to the ground in pain with a twisted knee. The network television announcers began predicting another Super Bowl blowout.

It turned out that their fears were well-founded, but it was not the Broncos who would dominate the game. A clue as to what could happen to Denver had come in the AFC championship game. In that game, the Bronco defense had totally collapsed after the offense had built a comfortable lead. Cleveland had

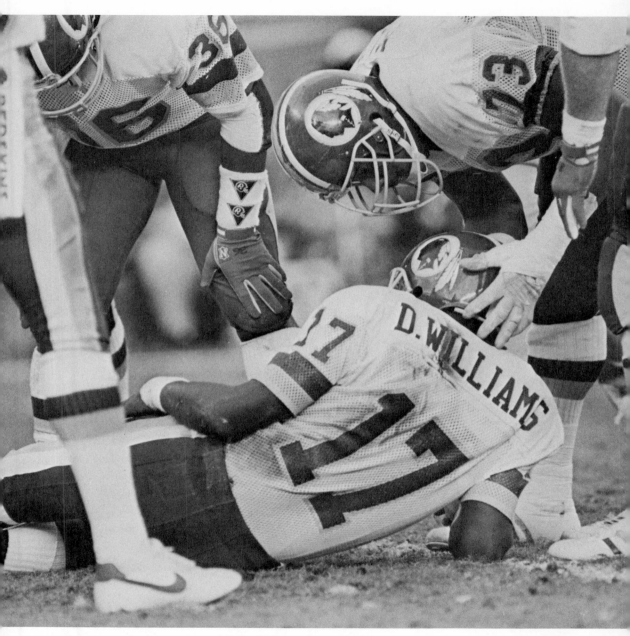

Teammates check on an injured Doug Williams during the first quarter of Super Bowl XXII. Despite twisting his knee, Williams returned to the game and turned in an MVP performance.

charged through the defenders at will, with a majority of the Browns' 464 yards coming in the second half. Obviously there were glaring weaknesses in Denver's defense. It would not be long before a determined Doug Williams would find them.

Williams hobbled back into the Redskins' lineup in the second quarter and ignited an aerial show. First, Ricky Sanders sprinted down the sideline with an 80-yard touchdown pass. Then Gary Clark worked free for a 27-yard touchdown catch. Timmy Smith burst through a huge hole created by the Hogs and galloped 58 yards for another score. As the Redskin offense piled up points, Washington's defensive pass rush grew ferocious. Elway could do nothing to move the Broncos downfield, and the hot Redskin offense kept scoring. Williams fired a pass to Sanders for a 50-yard touchdown and then closed out the half with an 8-yard scoring toss to Didier. Washington had pummeled the hapless Broncos for 35 points in a single quarter!

For all practical purposes, the game was over. In the second half, Elway was knocked down time after time, and Washington's Timmy Smith kept romping through the flimsy Bronco defense. Washington won, 42-10.

For the Redskins, the unheralded Smith finished the game with two touchdowns, and a record 204 yards

The Redskin defense stayed in John Elway's face all day, sacking him five times. Here, Dexter Manley closes in on the Bronco quarterback.

in 22 carries, an average of nearly 9 yards a try! Ricky Sanders also set a record with 193 yards on 9 catches. As in the previous Washington Super Bowl triumph, the Redskin defense thwarted the opposing quarterback. John Elway completed only 14 of 38 throws and was sacked 5 times.

The spotlight clearly belonged to Doug Williams. After two weeks of enduring questions about whether he had the talent to be a Super Bowl quarterback, Williams had given his answer on the football field. With 18 completions in 29 attempts for 340 yards and 4 touchdowns, Williams was a deserving winner of the MVP Award.

CHAPTER 2

Oakland/Los Angeles Raiders

Super Bowl XV
Super Bowl XVIII

Ever since Al Davis took over the team in 1963, the Oakland/Los Angeles Raiders have thrived on a reputation as a halfway house for society's outcasts. These renegades of the NFL paid little attention to ordinary standards of behavior in winning their first Super Bowl title in 1977. Their two championships in the '80s followed the same script.

General manager and owner Davis set a defiant tone by threatening to move his team from Oakland to Los Angeles in spite of league wishes. That led to lawsuits and charges and countercharges between Davis and NFL Commissioner Pete Rozelle. Eventually, the Raiders beat the system and moved to Los Angeles.

On the field, the Raiders sneered at the way most teams cautiously probed their opponents' defenses and looked to "take whatever the defense gives us." The Raiders brashly claimed that their offensive strategy was "to take whatever we want."

The Raiders acquired free-spirited players who had been trashed by other teams. Tops on this list of rusty, "washed up" players was quarterback Jim Plunkett. This college star had been shell-shocked because of poor pass protection at New England and San Francisco, and he no longer seemed capable of leading an offense. When even the lowly 49ers cut him in 1978, Plunkett's career seemed over. But the Raiders signed him and used him as a backup for a couple of years. When starting quarterback Dan Pastorini broke his leg early in the 1980 season, Plunkett was called back into action.

Oakland's top running back that year was Kenny King, salvaged from the Houston Oilers' bench. The defense relied on retreads such as linebackers Bob Nelson and Rod Martin. Both players had been cut by several teams. Burgess Owens started at safety after a lackluster career with the New York Jets. Nose tackle Reggie Kinlaw was a 12th-round draft choice, and many people considered him too small to play his position. With so many weak links in their lineup, the Raiders were picked by some experts to finish last in the division.

Instead, Plunkett experienced a miraculous rebirth. Protected by a wall of beefy linemen, he regained his touch as a dangerous passer. The defense, led by Ted Hendricks and Lester Hayes, was spectacular. Hendricks played roving linebacker. He disrupted offenses by charging in wherever he was least expected. Hayes, considered a weak cornerback by opposing teams the year before, bounced back to lead the league with 14 interceptions. These performances propelled Oakland into the play-offs with an 11-5 mark.

Because they were a wild-card team, the Raiders faced a tough trip to the Super Bowl, playing almost all the games on the road and having to play an extra game before the beginning of the play-offs. Wildcard teams play against each other to determine who advances to the second round to play against the division winners.

The Raiders were aided by a streak of luck in the play-offs. In the first game, Cleveland was well within range of a game-winning field goal in the final seconds, but chose to risk one more pass before kicking for the three points. Oakland's Mike Davis intercepted the pass, denying the Browns a chance at the

field goal and preserving a 14-12 win. The following week, against San Diego, a pass bounced off Kenny King into the arms of his teammate, Ray Chester. Chester scored on the broken play to provide the winning margin in a 34-27 win.

The Raiders faced a team with a completely opposite philosophy in Super Bowl XV at the New Orleans Superdome on January 25, 1981. Philadelphia Eagles Coach Dick Vermeil stressed

Jim Plunkett, right, confers with Coach Tom Flores, left, in the fourth quarter of Super Bowl XV. Plunkett seemed destined for a career as backup quarterback until an injury to Dan Pastorini put him into the starting lineup.

Raider linebacker Rod Martin picked off three passes in Super Bowl XV.

discipline. His practices had been the NFL's most punishing and had molded the players into a tough, determined team with no defensive weaknesses. Philadelphia's offense relied on the running of Wilbert Montgomery and the passing combination of Ron Jaworski and Harold Carmichael.

The Raiders continued to have good luck in the Super Bowl. Following a Rod Martin interception, Oakland's first drive was kept alive by an offsides penalty on the Eagles. Plunkett capped that drive with a 2-yard touchdown pass to Cliff Branch. Then a long Eagle touchdown pass to Rodney Parker was called back because of a motion penalty on Carmichael.

The key play of the game came when Plunkett had to run to escape a determined Eagle pass rush. After narrowly avoiding the sack, he found Kenny King all alone on the left sideline. King gathered in the pass and raced 80 yards for the score and a 14-0 lead. Meanwhile, the Raiders' tough defense against the run limited the Eagles to just one field goal in the first half.

In the second half, Plunkett calmly picked apart the Eagle defense. He capped one drive with a 29-yard pass to Branch, who stole the ball from defender Roynell Young at the goal line to increase the lead to 21-3. Plunkett then led the offense on two time-consuming marches that resulted in field goals.

Unheralded Rod Martin then demolished the last Eagle hopes by intercepting his second and third passes of the game. The Raiders coasted to a 27-10 victory.

Martin had a strong claim to the Most Valuable Player honor, except that the game was Jim Plunkett's finest hour. Plunkett had 13 completions in 21 attempts for 261 yards. In a year when the cast-off Raiders won the Super Bowl, it was fitting that Plunkett, the chief castoff, won the MVP award.

Several of the players returned to play key roles in the Raiders' next Super Bowl run in 1983. Jim Plunkett proved

The Raiders traded for veteran defensive end Lyle Alzado in 1982. He quickly became a key part of the team.

that his comeback year was not just a final hurrah. Rod Martin finally was gaining the respect that had been denied him so long. Todd Christensen, once cut by the Dallas Cowboys, had slowly established himself as the best tight end in football.

In addition, the Raiders had signed on another suspect character, brawler Lyle Alzado. The Cleveland Browns had traded this ferocious former All-Pro to the Raiders for a lowly ninth-round draft choice in 1982. Alzado's intimidating style fit so well with the free-spirit structure of the Raiders that he became a defensive leader. Alzado was voted the NFL's Comeback Player of the Year.

Al Davis' shrewd eye for talent unearthed another unheralded star in the 1981 draft. Davis used a second-round draft choice to select a player from a college that did not even have a football team! This player, 275-pound Howie Long, quickly developed into a dominating pass rusher. Davis was also one of the few people to recognize that Heisman Trophy winner Marcus Allen of the University of Southern California was really as good as his press clippings said he was. After many other teams passed up a chance to draft Allen in 1982, the Raiders grabbed him with their first-round selection.

Boasting their most talented roster in years, the Raiders posted a 8-1 record

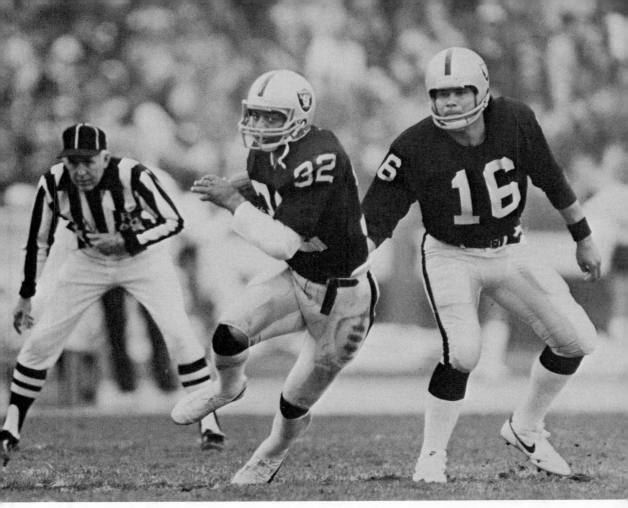

Running back Marcus Allen takes off after receiving a handoff from Plunkett.

in 1982, the best mark in the American Football Conference during a strike-shortened season. They lost, however, to the New York Jets early in the play-offs. That play-off loss seemed to underscore the Raiders' one glaring weakness —lack of a top-flight quarterback. In order for a team to win a Super Bowl, a strong performance at this position was necessary.

Veteran Jim Plunkett finally appeared to have outlived his usefulness in 1983. After a few substandard games, he was replaced in the starting lineup by young Marc Wilson. Wilson injured his shoulder in a game against Kansas City, however, and Plunkett was again pressed back into service.

That same month, November, the wily Al Davis engineered the move that may have clinched the title for team, which had moved to Los Angeles and changed its name to the Los Angeles Raiders. New England's All-Pro cornerback Mike Haynes had been sitting out the season because he was dissatisfied with his contract. Most teams were leery of pursuing a disgruntled player like Haynes, but Davis saw a golden opportunity. Recent rule changes on offensive holding and pass coverage had given offenses an advantage with the passing game. Teams were having great success with long passes to wide receivers. Suddenly it had become extremely important for a team to have two superb cornerbacks to cover those wide receivers.

The Raiders already had one outstanding cornerback in Lester Hayes. The addition of Mike Haynes would mean the Raiders could shut down those

Cornerback Lester Hayes helped the Raider defense contain opposing team's passing games in spite of new rules that benefited wide receivers.

Tight end Todd Christensen hauls in a pass during the Raiders' 38-10 win over the Pittsburgh Steelers in the play-offs.

high-powered passing attacks on both sides of the field. Davis went to work, and by the time he was done dealing, Haynes was wearing the silver and black of the Raiders.

By the end of the season, the Raiders were rampaging through their opponents from all directions. The amazing Plunkett recharged his throwing arm to pass for 20 touchdowns and nearly 3,000 yards. Todd Christensen set a team record with 92 catches, which was also the best in the league for the year. Marcus Allen rushed for 1,014 yards and added 590 more in pass receptions. Safety Vann McElroy tied for the AFC lead in interceptions with eight. Ted Hendricks saved a win against Kansas City with his 25th career block of a field-goal attempt.

As a team, the Raider offense led the AFC in points with 442, while the defense topped the NFL in sacks with 57, and allowed only 3.6 yards per rushing play. The result was a 12-4 record and a Western Division Championship.

This time, the Raiders refused to be sidetracked in the play-offs. First they pounded the Pittsburgh Steelers, 38-10, and then they rolled over the Seattle Seahawks by a score of 30-14.

Yet despite these impressive performances, the Raiders went into Super Bowl XVIII as the underdogs! Their opponents were the defending champion Washington Redskins, who had won 14 of their last 15 games and had scored an incredible 541 points during the season. Bruising back John Riggins had gotten 1,347 yards and 24 touchdowns, both Redskin records. Quarterback Joe Theismann had completed 60 percent of his passes for 29 touchdowns and only 11 interceptions. The Redskins had chewed up the Los Angeles Rams, 51-7, and held off the powerful San Francisco 49ers, 24-21, in the play-offs.

The Los Angeles Raiders had seen, firsthand, how explosive the Redskin offense could be. Early in the season, the Raiders had led the Redskins by a score of 35-20 with less than eight minutes remaining in the game. Yet Washington had stormed back to snatch a 37-35 victory.

Despite the experts' predictions, the Los Angeles Raiders never considered themselves underdogs. On January 22, 1984, in Tampa, Florida, the Raiders took the field confident that they would prevail. The coaching staff had observed a serious flaw in the Redskins' defense, which was ranked last in the league against the pass. The Raiders would strike deep.

Los Angeles also had a strategy for bottling up Washington's offense. Cornerbacks Hayes and Haynes would dismantle the Redskins' outside pass threats, Art Monk and Charlie Brown. Long and Alzado would lead a relentless pass rush. Nose tackle Reggie Kinlaw would drop off the line of scrimmage, and huge linebackers Matt Millen and Bob Nelson would crowd the Redskin guards to confuse them while they were trying to execute their run-blocking assignments.

It was neither the Raiders' strategy nor talent that rattled the Redskins early in the game, but rather a mistake. After their first offensive series was stopped, Washington sent in the punting team. One of the players missed a blocking assignment, though, because Derrick Jensen charged through the middle of the Redskin line untouched. Not only did he block the punt, but he pounced on the loose ball in the end zone. Suddenly, the Raiders had a 7-0 lead. Before the Redskins could regroup, Los Angeles had scored again. The big play

Derrick Jensen blocks the punt of Washington's Jeff Hayes early in Super Bowl XVIII. Jensen recovered the ball in the end zone for a Raider touchdown.

was a 50-yard pass from Plunkett to Cliff Branch. Branch finished off the drive with a 12-yard touchdown reception that gave the Raiders a surprising 14-0 lead.

Meanwhile, the potent Washington offense was sputtering. Reggie Kinlaw was playing the game of his life, shutting down Riggins and the running game. Haynes and Hayes were so effective at covering receivers that neither Monk nor Brown caught a pass in the first half.

The Redskin defense held fast, however, and late in the half, the Washington running game finally got untracked. A 13-play drive led to a field goal to cut the margin to 14-3, well within striking distance of the Raiders. A short time later, with the ball on Washington's 12-yard line and with only 12 seconds left in the half, the Redskins might have called a running play to get out of the half without further damage.

The Raider coaches suspected a trick, however. They remembered that in a similar situation when the two teams played earlier in the year, Washington had run a surprise play—a screen pass to shifty running back Joe Washington—that had gained 67 yards. The coaches sent in reserve linebacker Jack Squirek, a pass defense specialist, with instructions to follow Joe Washington. Sure enough, the Redskins tried the screen pass. Squirek was in position to make the interception and run into the end zone for a quick touchdown.

It was a critical mistake. Had the Redskins gone into the second half trailing by 11, they could have continued to use a balanced offensive attack. But down by 19, the team would have to take more chances and rely more and more on a risky passing game.

Plunkett's offensive line gave him plenty of time to find receivers.

Washington showed great patience early in the second half. With Riggins providing most of the power, the Redskins marched 70 yards for a touchdown. One short plunge by Riggins capped the best drive of the day. But any boost the Redskins might have received disappeared when the extra-point attempt was blocked.

The Raiders continued to attack with long passes, gaining 38 yards on a pass interference penalty on Redskin cornerback Darrell Green. The large gain set up a 5-yard touchdown run by Marcus Allen, who cut back to his left and slipped underneath several tacklers on his way to the end zone. With the Raiders leading, 28-9, Washington was desperate. Short yardage runs by Riggins would not get the Redskins the quick scores they needed to put themselves back in the game. The Los Angeles defensive unit could afford to concentrate less on Riggins and Washington's short-yardage game. The Raiders could instead unleash their fearsome pass rush.

Stubbornly, Washington advanced to the Raider 26-yard line late in the third quarter. Down by 19 points, there was no point in settling for a field goal. On fourth down and a yard to go, the coaching staff had sent in Riggins to pick up the first down behind blocking by the Hogs. Normally the Redskins excelled at short yardage situations, but Rod Martin and safety Mike Davis broke through the line to stop Riggins short of the first down.

On the last play of the quarter, Marcus Allen sealed the victory with a creative individual effort. Starting from his own 26, Allen took a pitch-out on a play that was designed to go to the left. Washington's Ken Coffey closed in from the left, however, so Allen stopped and circled to his right. Eluding the fast-closing Redskin tacklers, he burst through an opening in the middle of the field and outsprinted the defensive backs to the end zone. His 74-yard jaunt was the longest rushing score ever in Super Bowl action.

Chris Bahr later finished off the scoring with a 21-yard field goal to make the final score 38-9.

Marcus Allen had run so brilliantly, gaining 191 yards on just 20 carries, that he was an easy choice for the game's Most Valuable Player Award. Jim Plunkett had contributed a steady game with 16 completions in 25 attempts for 172 yards. Reggie Kinlaw had led the defensive charge that held Riggins to only 64 yards in 26 carries, and sacked Theismann six times. With the offense, the defense, and the special teams all scoring touchdowns, the big-play Raiders could truly say that Super Bowl XVIII was a team victory. As they had boasted, for one year anyway, the Raider attack squads had truly taken just about whatever they wanted.

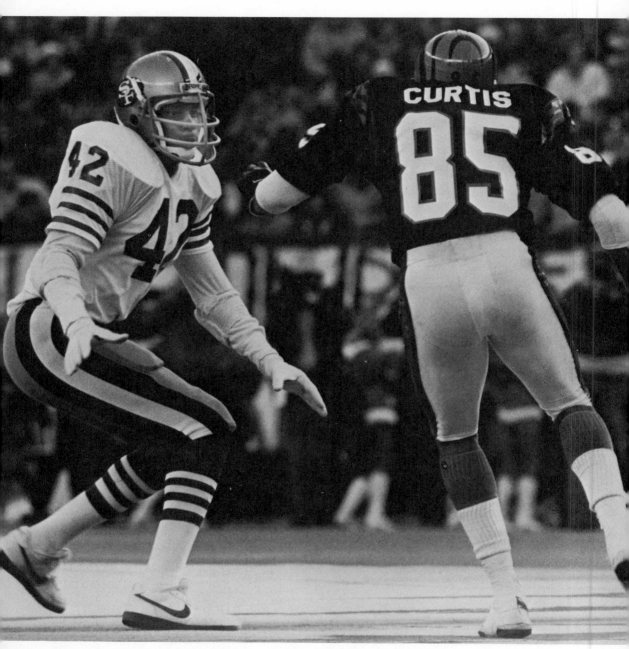

Cornerback Ronnie Lott was one of the 49ers who saw action in all of San Francisco's Super Bowl victories.

CHAPTER 3

San Francisco 49ers

Super Bowl XVI
Super Bowl XIX
Super Bowl XXIII
Super Bowl XXIV

The San Francisco 49ers' image was that of a far more civilized team than a one-time rival across the bay in Oakland. The difference was evident — brains over brawn, talent over intimidation, offense over defense, organization over reckless abandon. The 49ers seemed to be engineered rather than coached.

Unlike the other NFL champions of the '80s, the 49ers did not self-destruct after winning the Super Bowl. After San Francisco won Super Bowl XVI, some minor tinkering with the lineup produced yet another Super Bowl champion within three years. Even the departure of perfectionist Coach Bill Walsh after the 49ers' third Super Bowl victory did not derail the 49ers.

There was, however, one main part of the 49er machine that could not be replaced. San Francisco's offense relied on the cool head and precise arm of quarterback Joe Montana. In the 49ers' four Super Bowl wins, Montana was named the game's Most Valuable Player three times and nearly won it four times.

Actually, San Francisco's reputation as an offense-minded, finesse team was not entirely accurate. Teams seldom win football games without tough blocking on offense and aggressive tackling from the defense. But aside from hard-hitting defensive back Ronnie Lott, the 49ers did their work so quietly that they appeared to be merely a supporting cast in the "Joe Montana Show."

The engineer of the 49er dynasty was Bill Walsh. He arrived in San Francisco in 1979 to inherit one of the league's most pathetic teams. A former quarterback coach and offensive coordinator, Walsh was considered a genius at designing ways to score points. His game plan was so thoroughly organized that he knew, before each game started, exactly which plays the 49ers would use on their first 20 to 25 downs.

None of Walsh's expertise helped the

San Francisco Coach Bill Walsh designed an intricate offensive system for the 49ers.

In desperation, it seemed, the team rushed three rookies into the defensive backfield for the 1981 season, Lott, Eric Wright, and Carlton Williamson. Incredibly, the newcomers responded so well that the defensive backfield became one of the team's strong points in 1981. San Francisco plugged other defensive holes by signing Ram linebacker Jack Reynolds to stop the run and Charger All-Pro defensive end Fred Dean to boost the pass rush.

With 20 new players on the team, San Francisco posted a 13-3 mark, the best record in the league. The play-offs proved the 49ers were no fluke. In the NFC title game, Dwight Clark stretched high in the air to pull down a last-minute touchdown pass that beat the Cowboys, 28-27.

The 49ers' opponent in Super Bowl XVI on January 24, 1982, was the equally surprising Cincinnati Bengals. The Bengals' new striped helmets seemed to turn the slumbering Cincinnati club into ferocious players. Quarterback Ken Anderson, who had been one of the NFL's worst-ranked quarterbacks in 1980, captured his conference's Most Valuable Player Award. Beefy fullback Pete Johnson and skinny wide receiver Cris Collinsworth formed an unlikely offensive duo that led the Bengal attack. Linemen Ross Browner and Eddie Edwards powered a stingy defense. In winning the AFC title game, the Bengals

49ers much in his first two years as head coach. San Francisco won only two games in 1979 and six the following year. Joe Montana, a third-round draft choice out of Notre Dame, showed a knack for picking up Walsh's system and for performing under pressure. The 49ers also had a handful of other promising players, but the defense was lousy. San Francisco defensive backs allowed opponents to complete two-thirds of their passes in 1980.

held San Diego's high-powered offense to seven points, logging a 27-7 victory.

Fans in Detroit's Silverdome were just settling back to watch the game when disaster struck the 49ers. "Famous Amos" Lawrence fumbled the opening kickoff, and the Bengals recovered the ball at San Francisco's 26-yard line. It looked as though Cincinnati would pick up an early score, but San Francisco's defensive backs came to the rescue. Dwight Hicks, the only veteran in the defensive backfield, stepped in front of Cincinnati's Isaac Curtis to intercept a pass near the goal line.

Montana then sprung Walsh's clever game plan on the bewildered Bengals. The 49ers marched steadily downfield, using a variety of strange formations and newly invented pass patterns. Montana finished the 68-yard drive by diving into the end zone from the 1-yard line.

Cincinnati's next threat was again thwarted by the 49er defensive backs. Eric Wright stripped Collinsworth of the ball on a pass completion at the 8-yard line, and San Francisco recovered. This time, San Francisco traveled 92 yards for the score, mixing passes,

Cincinnati Coach Forrest Gregg jokes with quarterback Ken Anderson (14), tight end Dan Ross (89), and running back Pete Johnson (46) during pre-game warmups on the day of the Super Bowl.

Fullback Earl Cooper hauls in a pass from Joe Montana. Cooper took the ball into the end zone to give the 49ers a 14-0 lead.

runs, and trick plays to perfection. Running back Earl Cooper made a fine grab of a high pass to cover the final 11 yards and build the lead to 14-0.

Ken Anderson had trouble dodging Fred Dean and the rest of the 49er pass rushers. Cincinnati's failure to move the ball gave San Francisco another opportunity to pad the lead. Ray Wersching kicked a field goal just before halftime. On the following kickoff, Cincinnati running back Archie Griffin dropped the ball, and other players bobbled it while trying to pick it up. San Francisco recovered the fumble, and Wersching stayed on the field to kick yet another field goal before time ran out in the half.

With the score 20-0, it looked like the usual dull Super Bowl mismatch until the Bengals started the second half looking like a different team. Anderson picked up the Bengals' first touchdown with a dash into the end zone from 5 yards away.

Then the Bengals drove for a first down on the 49er 3-yard line. From there Pete Johnson hurled his 258 pounds into the line and barreled down to the 1. The Bengals sent Johnson into the line again, but this time he was stopped by Reynolds for no gain. A third-down pass play to halfback Charles Alexander was foiled by linebacker Dan Bunz, who tackled Alexander short of the end zone.

Facing a fourth down, just inches from the goal line, Bengals' Coach Forrest Gregg elected to try for the touchdown. No one, least of all the 49ers, was surprised when Johnson got the ball. The fullback was stacked up short of the line of scrimmage to halt the Bengals' momentum.

Undaunted, Cincinnati fought back for a fourth-period touchdown. Tight end Dan Ross, enjoying a fine game, scored on a 4-yard touchdown pass to make it 20-14.

With the lead dwindling, the 49er offense and the defensive backs resumed their first-half heroics. Linemen Randy Cross and Keith Fahnhorst paved the way for the San Francisco running game. The 49ers moved the ball downfield, and Wersching kicked a field goal. Eric Wright's interception and return set up another Wersching kick.

Anderson and Ross stormed downfield for Cincinnati, but their last-minute touchdown could only close the gap. San Francisco held on to win, 26 to 21.

Joe Montana had played coolly for a young quarterback, completing 14 of 22 passes for 157 yards. Although those were fairly modest statistics, they were enough to win him Most Valuable Player honors. However, the defense provided most of the heroics, with five sacks, two interceptions, a fumble recovery, and a thrilling goal-line stand.

After a disappointing 1982 season, Coach Walsh decided that Montana needed some more weapons in his offensive arsenal. In 1983, he traded for Los Angeles Ram running back Wendell Tyler, a talented runner who had been bumped out of the Rams' plans by top draft-choice Eric Dickerson. At the same time, he drafted a 6-foot, 220-pound blocking back from Nebraska, Roger Craig, to help clear the way for Tyler. Craig surprised the 49ers by doing more than blocking. With his speed, powerful running ability, and pass-catching skills, Craig quickly developed into one of the league's best all-purpose backs.

Even with this bolstered running game, San Francisco could not unseat reigning NFC champion Washington during the 1983 season. Walsh decided that the 49ers needed to improve their pass rush to get back to the top. Back in 1981 Walsh had bolstered his pass rush by trading for San Diego's ferocious Fred Dean, and had gone on to win the Super Bowl. This time, though, there was no one of Dean's caliber available. In a daring move, Walsh decided to make up for quality with quantity. In 1984 Walsh obtained two of Dean's old San Diego pass-rushing mates, Gary "Big Hands" Johnson and Louie Kelcher, picked up Manu Tuiasosopo from Seattle, and drafted huge shot put champion Michael Carter. Along with Dean, Dwaine Board, Jeff Stover, Lawrence Pillers, and Jim Stuckey, the new players brought San Francisco's defensive linemen count to nine, two or three more than most teams had! Walsh substituted frequently among the linemen, keeping them fresh and using players as their strengths fit a particular situation.

Walsh's red-and-gold machine performed almost flawlessly during the 1984 season. The offensive attack was so balanced that Wendell Tyler was able to gain a team-record 1,262 yards rushing in the same year that Montana led the league in passing! With place-kicker Ray Wersching adding a team-record 131 points and the defense ranked as the stingiest in the league, it was no wonder that San Francisco won 15 times in 16 games. Only a determined Pittsburgh Steeler team kept the 49ers from an undefeated season.

In the play-offs, the 49er offense coasted while the defense enjoyed some rare moments in the spotlight. The defense allowed only one field goal in a 21-10 victory over the New York Giants, then recorded 9 sacks in a 23-0 thrashing of the Chicago Bears in the NFC title game.

The team's season-long display of power, however, got lost in the fireworks exploding in Miami. In only his second season in the pros, Dolphins' quarterback Dan Marino had shattered several quarterback records. Some starting pro quarterbacks can play an entire season and complete no more than 12 touchdown passes. In 1984 Marino threw for 12 touchdown passes after he had already tied the NFL record of 36 touchdown passes in a season! Marino completed an astounding 362 passes for 5,034 yards. Nearly 2,700 of those yards had come on passes to speedy wide receivers Mark Clayton and Mark Duper.

In the play-offs, the Dolphin attack had been unstoppable. Miami had warmed up for the Super Bowl by beating the Seattle Seahawks, 31-10. Then Marino had dominated Pittsburgh in the championship, passing for 421

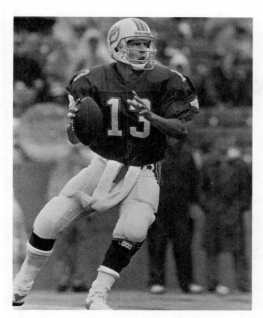

Miami quarterback Dan Marino was the talk of the NFL in 1984.

yards and 4 touchdowns in just 32 pass attempts. There seemed to be no way to stop him. Marino read defenses so well and passed the ball so quickly that even blitzing did not work against him.

The 49ers, tired of hearing about how spectacular the Dolphins were, looked forward to Super Bowl Sunday on January 20, 1985, in Palo Alto, California. The San Francisco players were well aware that Miami's Killer Bees defense (9 of the 11 starters had last names beginning with *B*) had shown a weakness all year against the run. They also knew that Miami did not have much of a running game to go with the

incredible passing attack. That meant that the 49ers had to prepare only for the Miami passing game, while the Dolphins would have to defend against San Francisco's more balanced attack.

In the first series of the Super Bowl, Marino lived up to all the advance billing. Darting his passes between the 49er defenders, he drove the Dolphins far enough to set up a 37-yard field goal by Uwe von Schamann.

Joe Montana, however, was not ready to concede that Marino was the best quarterback on the field. Facing a third-and-7 near midfield, Montana kept the drive alive by scrambling away from a heavy pass rush for a 15-yard gain. On the next play, he connected with reserve running back Carl Monroe on a 33-yard touchdown pass to give San Francisco a 7-3 lead.

The Dolphins came back with a no-huddle offense. Marino completed five passes in a row. A 2-yard touchdown pass to tight end Dan Johnson put Miami back on top, 10-7.

After watching Marino chew up his regular defense, Coach Walsh made a drastic change. San Francisco's basic defense was a 3-4-4 alignment, using three defensive linemen, four linebackers, and four defensive backs. Daring the Dolphins to run, San Francisco put in an "elephant" defense—a 4-2-5 alignment that was normally used only in certain passing situations. Tom Holmoe

San Francisco adjusted its defense early in the game to get through the offensive line, and at Marino, faster.

went in as a fifth defensive back in place of a linebacker and Jeff Fuller, a large defensive back, took over one of the other linebacking spots. A third linebacker was replaced by Big Hands Johnson. The 49ers hoped that Johnson could provide a strong pass rush up the middle and get in Marino's face before the quarterback could set up to throw. That would buy enough time for

Fred Dean, Dwaine Board, and the other linemen to break through for the sack.

The change worked. Marino, who had completed 9 of 10 passes against the regular defense, began to struggle. In the meantime, Montana and Roger Craig were shredding the Killer Bee defense. In the second quarter, Montana flipped a touchdown pass to Craig, carried the ball 6 yards for another score, and handed off to Craig, who burst in for a third touchdown from 2 yards out. With time running out in the first half, San Francisco was ahead 28-10 and appeared to be coasting to an easy win.

Marino, who continued to pass on almost every down, rallied the Dolphins into position for a field goal with 12 seconds remaining in the half. Von Schamann came through again to cut the lead to 15 points. On the kickoff, San Francisco blocker Guy McIntyre was confused by conflicting advice from his teammates. Rather than simply falling on the ball so that the 49ers could run out the clock, McIntyre tried to run with it. He fumbled, Miami's Jim Jensen recovered, and von Schamann booted yet another field goal to put Miami back into contention, 28-16.

In the second half, however, it was clear that Marino had finally run into a defense he could not solve. Miami's lack of a running attack allowed the 49er linemen to charge recklessly after

the passer. Big Hands Johnson exploded through the middle of Miami's heralded offensive line to send Marino ducking for cover. Under pressure from San Francisco's elephant defense, Marino was sacked four times and completed only 11 of 30 passes. Two of his throws were intercepted, including a touchdown-saving effort in the third quarter by Eric Wright.

While Marino was taking a pounding, Montana and his squad were padding their statistics at the expense of the bewildered Dolphin defense. In contrast to Miami's one-dimensional attack, San Francisco's balanced blend of passing, running, and scrambling kept the defenders off balance. Taking advantage of subpar punts by Miami's Reggie Roby, San Francisco tacked on a 27-yard field goal by Wersching and a 16-yard touchdown pass from Montana to Craig in the third quarter.

Comfortably ahead, 38-16, the 49ers were content to kill time for the rest of the game. Miami mounted no further threat, and San Francisco breezed to a win. The final statistics were a grim monument to another one-sided Super Bowl. The 49ers racked up 31 first downs and 537 total yards, both Super Bowl records. Roger Craig set another mark with three touchdowns, and Montana claimed yet another with his 331 yards worth of pass offense.

While Craig had a strong claim on

the game's MVP Award, Montana captured the honor for the second time in his career. By completing 24 of 35 passes and rushing for 59 yards, he had shown that it was too early to concede that Dan Marino was the best quarterback in football.

Neither Montana nor Marino made it back to the NFL's showcase game the next three seasons, though. As the 49ers fizzled again and again in the play-offs, Montana's reputation as a big-game quarterback began to suffer. The 49ers were humiliated by the Giants in the 1986 play-offs, and then thrashed by the underdog Vikings in 1987. In the latter game, Montana played so poorly that he was benched in favor of reserve Steve Young.

It did not appear that San Francisco would even make the play-offs after the 1988 season. At one point, the 49ers were only 6-5 and trailed both the Saints and Rams in their own division. Both the offensive and defensive lines were being rebuilt, and the inexperience showed. Montana, who had suffered a serious back injury the previous year, seemed in danger of being replaced by the younger, more mobile Steve Young.

San Francisco recovered, however, to claim the Western Division championship. Although still famous for precision passing wizardry, the 49ers relied more on muscle than on passing. Led by Roger Craig, who finished second in

With Montana slowed by injuries and seemingly becoming less effective, Steve Young took over the starting quarterback spot for the 49ers during the regular season. Montana had the job back before the season was over.

the NFC with 1,502 yards rushing, San Francisco boasted the best rushing attack in the National Football Conference.

The smooth, high-stepping running back also was an important part of the 49ers' passing attack. Craig ranked fifth in the conference in pass receiving with 76 catches for 534 yards. Third-year wide receiver Jerry Rice grabbed 64 passes for 1,306 yards and 9 touchdowns. Montana, meanwhile, survived weak pass protection to rank sixth in the league in passing.

As the play-offs approached, Montana was constantly reminded of his recent history of failure in big games. This time, he took charge as the 49ers dominated two strong teams to win the NFC championship. First San Francisco

beat the Vikings, 34 to 9, and then pounded the Bears, 28 to 3. In both games, the unheralded 49er defense, led by pass-rushing linebacker Charles Haley, shut down powerful offensive teams.

On the strength of those two impressive wins, San Francisco was a strong favorite over AFC champion Cincinnati. The Bengals, however, featured a double-barrel attack similar to what San Francisco had brought into their last Super Bowl game. The similarities between the two offenses were more than a coincidence. Cincinnati head

Below: The newly built Joe Robbie Stadium in Miami was the site of Super Bowl XXIII.

coach Sam Wyche had, several years earlier, been a quarterback coach for Bill Walsh's 49ers.

Cincinnati could grind away at opponents with a punishing running attack or strike quickly with passes. Few opponents were able to stop both methods. Quarterback Boomer Esiason led the entire NFL in passing, with swift Eddie Brown as his favorite target. At the same time, the Bengals also ranked as the league's top rushing team. Powerful rookie fullback Ickey Woods and shifty little veteran James Brooks combined for nearly 2,000 rushing yards behind a mountainous offensive line.

The Bengals' defense was not nearly as well-respected. Led by All-Pro nose tackle Tim Krumrie and safety David Fulcher, however, Cincinnati had held both play-off opponents to fewer than 14 points.

On January 22, 1989, the teams met at Joe Robbie Stadium in Miami. The game opened with the sloppiness and bad fortune that had plagued many Super Bowl games. Early in the first quarter, the 49ers lost tackle Steve Wallace to an injury. Minutes later, Cincinnati's Krumrie broke his leg while making a tackle and had to be carried off the field.

San Francisco's first serious drive was ensnarled in the controversial instant-replay rule. Officials on the field ruled that Montana's 22-yard pass to Mike Wilson was complete, which would have given the 49ers a first down near the Bengal goal line. Upon further review, though, officials in the replay booth determined that Wilson never had control of the ball. San Francisco had to settle for a 41-yard field goal from the NFC's leading scorer, place-kicker Mike Cofer. A short time later, the 49ers lost three points when a short field-goal attempt was botched because of a poor snap from center Randy Cross.

Cincinnati's polished offensive unit could do no better in the first half, scoring its only points on a 34-yard field goal by Jim Breech. The Bengals stayed close largely on big plays by safety David Fulcher, who stripped Roger Craig of the ball to stop one drive and contributed timely tackles on other occasions.

Neither quarterback had shown championship qualities in the first 30 minutes. Montana was having trouble reading the defenses. Esiason's passes were seldom on target. All in all, it was a poor exhibition of football, even when compared to the lax standards of the Super Bowl.

The action began to heat up, though, in the second half. Esiason finally connected with Cris Collinsworth on two passes to set up a 43-yard field goal by Breech. San Francisco reserve linebacker Bill Romanowski then gave his

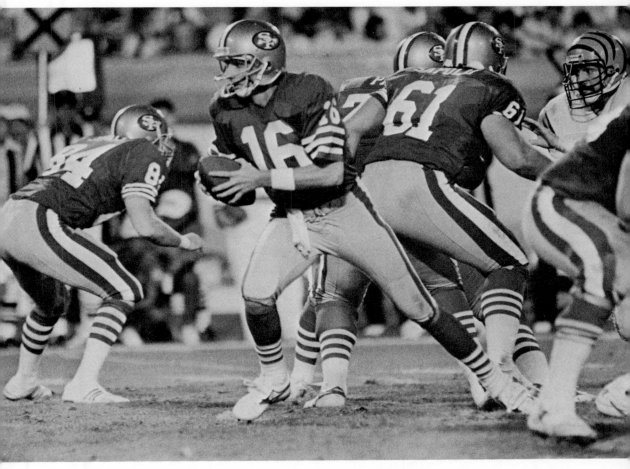

Montana looks to hand off while his blockers keep the Cincinnati defense away.

team a much needed lift. Using every inch of his 6-foot, 4-inch height, he tipped an Esiason pass and pulled it in for an interception that set up a 32-yard field goal by Cofer.

On the kickoff, Cincinnati's Stanford Jennings jolted the crowd with the game's first touchdown, a 93-yard kick-off return. A suddenly aroused 49er offense barged down the field deep into Bengal territory at the start of the fourth quarter. Cincinnati came agonizingly close to sealing the victory when a Montana pass sailed right into the hands of Bengal cornerback Lewis Billups in the end zone. Billups could not hold on, however. Given another chance, Montana drilled a more accurate toss to Jerry Rice, who barely squeezed into the end zone before being knocked out of bounds. The score was tied again, 13-13.

For the first time in the game, the brawny Cincinnati blockers began blasting paths for Ickey Woods. The Bengals charged down to the 49er 22-yard line before settling for a Breech field goal and a 16-13 lead.

A holding penalty on the ensuing kickoff buried the 49ers deep in their own territory. With only 3:20 left to play, San Francisco was 92 yards away from a winning touchdown. Even Montana was thinking more about getting in position for a game-tying field goal than going for a touchdown. Facing a Bengal defense that now included six defensive backs to prevent the 49ers from completing a deep pass, Montana went to work. A few short passes and

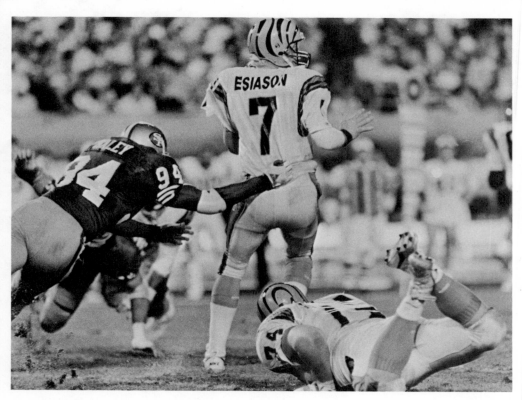

Under pressure from San Francisco linebacker Charles Haley, Boomer Esiason searches downfield for an open receiver.

Wide receiver John Taylor became a hero when he caught the game-winning touchdown pass with less than a minute remaining in Super Bowl XXIII.

Bengal 45 with less than a minute left. Montana looked for his ace receiver, Jerry Rice, who had enjoyed a spectacular game so far. Rice not only made the catch in heavy traffic, but he escaped several tacklers to pick up a first down. After another short pass to Craig, the 49ers had reached the Bengal 10 with the clock ticking down to about 30 seconds. Montana looked for Craig up the middle, but Craig had been held up at the line of scrimmage. Quickly, Montana shifted his sights to his second target, reserve receiver John Taylor, in the left side of the end zone. Taylor was there and open. Montana's pass was on target, and the 49ers had pulled out a thrilling win.

In the end, the 49er superstars had come through. Roger Craig gained 74 yards rushing and caught eight passes for 101 yards, with many of those yards on the final drive. Joe Montana had provided cool leadership under enormous pressure and finished with a Super Bowl-record 357 yards passing. Either one would have been a deserving choice for MVP. However, the award went to Jerry Rice, who had outfoxed the Bengal defense for 11 catches worth a Super Bowl-record 215 yards. The game had been one of the most exciting Super Bowls ever.

Not since the 1979 Pittsburgh Steelers had any NFL champion successfully defended its title. If the 49ers were to

runs up the middle got the team some breathing room. Patiently, Montana completed more short passes as the clock wound down to the final minute.

Unfortunately, a holding penalty left the 49ers with a second-and-20 on the break this string in 1989, they would have to do it under the leadership of a rookie head coach. Bill Walsh retired following his third Super Bowl win, and defensive coordinator George Seifert replaced him.

Seifert's laid-back style concerned some of the San Francisco veterans at first, but it quickly became apparent that he was in control as firmly as Walsh had been. He had a roster full of veterans determined to repeat as Super Bowl champions.

As important as he had been to the team's previous success, Joe Montana became the absolute master of the gridiron. At the age of 33, he racked up the highest efficiency rating of any quarterback in history. Montana completed more than 70 percent of his passes in 1989, throwing for 26 touchdowns and giving up only 8 interceptions. The Philadelphia Eagles learned first-hand about Montana's clutch performances. After three quarters of being pounded by the fierce Eagle pass rush, Montana hurled four fourth-quarter touchdown passes to pull out a victory.

Jerry Rice was Montana's main target, leading the NFL with 1,483 yards receiving and 17 touchdowns. John Taylor took advantage of the attention given Rice by defenses to catch 60 passes for 1,077 yards and 10 touchdowns.

Roger Craig again provided much of the legwork, with 1,054 yards rushing and 1,527 total yards. His burden was eased by a former teammate at the University of Nebraska, burly Tom Rathman. Rathman caught 73 passes coming out of the backfield, for 616 yards.

The defense was a typical, low-key 49er unit, held together by Ronnie Lott. Charles Haley led the pass rush, Raider castoff Matt Millen stuffed the opposing running game, and Don Griffin provided All-Pro cornerback coverage.

Perhaps San Francisco's most innovative move was the use of platoon players. With nose tackle Michael Carter injured much of the year, battle-scarred veterans Pete Kugler and Jim Burt took turns filling the void. San Francisco got better production from enormous offensive tackle Bubba Paris when he alternated quarters with Steve Wallace. Bruce Collie played the first and third quarter of every game, while Terry Tausch handled quarters two and four.

San Francisco breezed through the regular season with a 14-2 mark. As the play-offs approached, the 49ers obviously had their eyes on only one thing: the Super Bowl. Montana played flawlessly in the play-offs, intimidating rival quarterbacks into subpar games. His task was simplified by the unexpected brilliance of the offensive line. A unit that had allowed 45 sacks during the season suddenly formed a concrete wall around their quarterback. With plenty of time to survey the field, Montana carved up the Vikings' top-rated defense, 41-13, and then ground up the Rams, 30-3, to get San Francisco in the Super Bowl for the fourth time.

The other Super Bowl team, the Denver Broncos, was also making its fourth Super Bowl appearance. While San Francisco had won in all of its previous Super Bowls, Denver had yet to win one. The team had looked impressive during the regular season, clinching the divisional title shortly after midseason. Quarterback John Elway came off a mediocre season to wallop the Browns in the AFC championship game, 37-21. After passing for 385 yards against Cleveland, Elway had hopes of being able to match Joe Montana. Denver had other offensive weapons in rookie running back Bobby Humphrey, who rushed for 1,151 yards in the regular season, and wide receiver Vance Johnson, who gained 1,095 yards on pass receptions.

The Bronco defense was much larger and more ferocious than past Denver defenses. Simon Fletcher led the team with 12 sacks. Hard-hitting safeties Steve Atwater and Dennis Smith spearheaded the pass defense. Denver had not given up more than 28 points in any game. The players were confident that their aggressive safeties could give the 49er receivers a tough game.

With plenty of room in front of him, Jerry Rice makes an over-the-shoulder catch during Super Bowl XXIV.

On January 28, 1990, the two squads met in the Louisiana Superdome. The early signs were bad for the Broncos. Elway's passes were off target, and Vance Johnson dropped the balls that did reach him. The 49ers wasted no time in putting together a precise, methodical drive. With an uncanny knack for converting nearly every third down into a first down, the 49ers drove to the Bronco 20. Jerry Rice then grabbed a Montana pass and spun away from a defender for a touchdown.

Denver fought back with some hard running by Bobby Humphrey, who was playing with injured ribs, to pick up a field goal and cut the gap to 7-3. After stopping the 49ers' next possession, Denver took over near midfield, in great shape to add points. Again, the Broncos went to Humphrey on the first play. San Francisco defenders Kevin Fagan and Chet Brooks hit Humphrey near the line of scrimmage, causing him to fumble the ball. San Francisco recovered and, for all practical purposes, the game was over.

Montana finished the quarter with a 7-yard touchdown pass to tight end Brent Jones to put the 49ers ahead, 13-3. With Elway repeatedly misfiring for Denver, San Francisco kept getting the ball back. Craig and Rathman took turns rushing the ball on the next drive. Rathman capped the drive with a 1-yard run into the end zone to make the score 20-3. Just before halftime, Rice streaked past the Denver safeties to haul in a 38-yard touchdown pass for a 27-3 lead.

Elway, who had completed only 6 of 20 passes in the first half, started the second half by throwing straight to San Francisco's Mike Walter. On Denver's second series of the half, he tossed another interception. Montana, with good protection from his offensive line, kept

exploiting the weakness in the Bronco's middle defense. First Rice, and then Taylor, dashed untouched into the end zone on long routes past the safeties.

With the game out of reach at 41-3, Denver finally moved the ball. There was little reason to celebrate, though, after Elway's 3-yard touchdown run cut the gap to 41-10. Elway's success was momentary. Before long, he had fumbled the ball deep in his own territory. Rathman and Craig finished off the scoring with a pair of short touchdown runs early in the fourth quarter. The

Running back Roger Craig cuts into a hole while carrying the ball against the Broncos.

— 48 —

final score was 55-10, and it could easily have been much worse!

The usual heroes had come through with fine performances. Craig, despite battling the flu, turned in a fine performance, with 69 yards rushing and 34 yards on pass receptions. Rice dazzled the crowd with 7 catches for 148 yards and three touchdowns. Rathman scored twice, caught 4 passes and ran for 38 yards.

San Francisco's defense had allowed the Broncos only 167 total yards, 99 of them by Humphrey, and had intercepted two passes and recovered two fumbles. Denver quarterbacks were sacked six times and held to only 11 completions in 29 pass attempts.

But all of the defense's efforts were overshadowed by Montana's finest hour. His three play-off games were as close to flawless as any quarterback has played. In the first halves of those games, when the outcomes were still slightly in doubt, Montana completed a total of 46 out of 58 passes for 597 yards and nine touchdowns with no interceptions.

Montana's statistics for this Super Bowl showed 22 completions in 29 throws for 297 yards and five touchdowns. That was easily enough to earn him his third Super Bowl Most Valuable Player Award. It also gave him every Super Bowl record that a quarterback could achieve, including 122 consecutive passes without an interception.

By the game's end, there was no doubt that the San Francisco 49ers were the NFL's Team of the Decade and that quarterback Joe Montana was the Player of the Decade.

Patriot Irving Fryar slips away from Chicago's Dennis Gentry in Super Bowl XX.

CHAPTER 4

Chicago Bears

Super Bowl XX

For many years it had been Walter Payton against the world. As splendid an athlete as he was, the NFL's all-time leading rusher could not win a title by himself. Year after year, Payton ran hard, the Chicago Bears defense played rough, and the team's fans went home disappointed.

Chicago General Manager Jim Finks refused to panic. Patiently he used the draft to collect top-quality players to fill out the Bear team. It was not until 1985, near the end of Payton's career, that the Chicago Bears finally stockpiled enough talent to win a Super Bowl. But when they did, they made it worth the wait for Bear fans who had not experienced as much as a conference title since 1963. The brash, outspoken Bears roared through their schedule. Seldom, if ever, has the NFL seen a more outrageous cast of characters than the colorful bunch that dominated the NFL in 1985.

Payton had already rushed for more than 5,000 yards in four seasons by the time Chicago used two first-round draft choices to shore up the defensive line in 1979. Dan Hampton of Arkansas provided the Bears with a ferocious inside pass rush, while Arizona State's Al Harris was a versatile end/linebacker. In 1980, Chicago drafted aggressive linebacker Otis Wilson and hard-nosed fullback Matt Suhey. Tackle Keith Van Horne and ferocious middle linebacker Mike Singletary were the top choices the following year.

Despite these impressive newcomers, Chicago finished with only 6 wins in 16 games in 1981. Desperate for some fresh leadership, the Bears drafted quarterback Jim McMahon of Brigham Young the next season and hired a tough new head coach, Mike Ditka. But the Bears continued to flounder, winning only three of nine games in a strike-shortened season.

Stubbornly sticking to a strategy of building through the draft, the Bears hit the jackpot in 1983. When draft day was over, three offensive linemen (Jim Covert, Tom Thayer, and Mark Bortz), a game-breaking wide receiver (Willie Gault), two defensive backs (Mike Richardson and Dave Duerson), and a devastating pass rusher (Richard Dent) had all been added to the Bear roster.

That left only a few weak links in the team's lineup. These were patched up, again using the draft. Linebacker Wilber Marshall arrived in 1984, and

defensive tackle William Perry and placekicker Kevin Butler reported for duty in 1985.

On the very first day of 1985 practice, Defensive Coordinator Buddy Ryan stirred up controversy by fuming that rookie Perry was a wasted draft choice. From that time on, the Bear camp was a news reporter's dream. The gruff Ryan feuded with hot-tempered Head Coach Ditka, who frequently raged at his players. Al Harris and hard-hitting

Chicago's backfield of Walter Payton, left, and Matt Suhey, right, gave the Bears an excellent running game to go with an effective passing game.

safety Todd Bell refused to accept the contracts offered by Bear management and sat out the season. Quarterback Jim McMahon, sporting wild sunglasses, punk hairdos, and a stubborn streak of independence, became an instant celebrity.

But the most bizarre situation of all concerned 300-pound William "The Refrigerator" Perry. A tremendous athlete despite his bulk, Perry offered Coach Ditka a chance for revenge on the 49ers. In the NFC championship game the previous year, San Francisco had used a 270-pound offensive lineman as a blocking back. After defeating the Bears, 23-0, the 49ers had also rubbed it in by saying, "Next time, bring an offense."

When the two teams played early in 1985, Ditka gave the 49ers a bigger dose of their own medicine. Late in the game, which the Bears won handily, The Refrigerator entered the game as the world's largest running back. Perry performed well enough that Ditka occasionally played him at that position.

In a Monday night game against the Packers, The Refrigerator had fans howling in delight as he lumbered into the end zone for a score. Almost overnight, The Refrigerator became pro football's biggest celebrity.

Amid all these distractions, the Bears demolished one opponent after another. With Payton leading the way, as usual, the Bears led the league in rushing. McMahon provided much-needed leadership at quarterback and kept defenses honest with long bombs to Willie Gault.

It was the Bear defense, however, that really terrorized opponents. Chicago used a unique "46" defense that put two outside linebackers side-by-side in front of the opposing tight end. Rushing as many as nine people from all different angles, the Bears made life miserable for quarterbacks. With the NFL's Defensive Player of the Year, Mike Singletary, directing the complex defense, Chicago allowed an average of fewer than 13 points per game in posting a 15-1 record.

During the play-offs, the Bears shifted into an even higher gear. First, Chicago blanked the New York Giants, 21-0, and shut out the Los Angeles Rams, who scraped together only 130 yards of offense the entire game. As the Bears traveled to New Orleans for the Super Bowl, the players were looking for a third straight play-off shutout.

Standing in the way of that goal on January 26, 1986, were the New England Patriots. The surprising Patriots had forced turnovers and relied almost exclusively on a powerful running game to get to the Super Bowl. New England had caused six turnovers in a 27-20 win over the Raiders and six more in a 31-14 win over Miami.

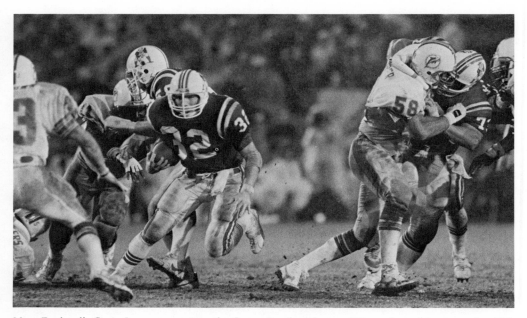

New England's Craig James came into the Super Bowl with over 100 yards rushing in each of his last two games, including this win over Miami in the AFC title game.

Quarterback Tony Eason had averaged only 13 passes in the two games, while running back Craig James and an offensive line averaging nearly 280 pounds had done the rest of the work. Unfortunately for New England, no one had yet figured out a way to run against Chicago's line-crowded defense. In beating New England 20-7 earlier in the year, Chicago had allowed the Patriots only 27 yards rushing. New England had a choice of running into the tough Bear defense or trying a passing game — a weak aspect of the offense.

Chicago's goal of a shutout was snuffed on the second play of the game.

Quarterback McMahon's mistake in play-calling led to a mixup and a fumble by Payton. New England recovered on the Bear 19, well within field-goal range. Choosing the element of surprise, Eason threw three quick passes. None was complete, and Tony Franklin came on to kick a 36-yard field goal.

Then the nightmare began. A 43-yard pass from McMahon to Gault set up a 28-yard field goal by Butler to tie the score. On New England's next possession, Chicago's Richard Dent and Steve McMichael burst through the line to knock the ball away from Tony Eason. Dan Hampton recovered for the Bears at the New England 13. Fighting valiantly to stop the Bears' momentum, the Patriot defense held fast, and the Bears were forced to settle for another Butler field goal, and a 6-3 lead.

On the first play after the kickoff, however, the Patriots again ran into Richard Dent. This time the Bear defensive end stripped the ball from Craig James. Singletary pounced on it, and again the Bears took over deep in New England territory.

Seeing that the Patriots were concentrating on stopping Walter Payton, Chicago crossed the defense up by sending fullback Matt Suhey straight ahead. Suhey churned 11 yards to the end zone for a 13-3 Chicago lead.

For the rest of the half, the Patriots found that moving the ball against the Bears was like trying to row against a tidal wave. None of New England's first plays in nine possessions was able to advance the ball a single inch! Chicago took advantage of good field position to mount another scoring drive early in the second quarter.

Continuing a season-long series of bizarre innovations, Chicago sent in a play in which The Refrigerator was supposed to roll out and throw a pass. Seeing that no one was open, however, Perry wisely passed up his chance to become pro football's largest passer and instead was sacked for a short loss. Again using Payton as a decoy,

McMahon carried the ball the final 2 yards for the score.

In the second quarter, trailing 20-3, New England Coach Ray Berry replaced shell-shocked starting quarterback Eason with veteran Steve Grogan. At that point, Eason had failed to complete a single pass in six attempts and had been sacked three times.

Grogan's luck was not much better. New England went into the locker room down, 23-3, after Butler had padded the lead on another short field goal. The Patriot offense had been stifled. Rather than gaining any yardage, New England had lost ground. The statistics

Placekicker Kevin Butler

William "The Refrigerator" Perry, normally a defensive lineman, became a running back on this play to score a short-yardage touchdown for the Bears.

at halftime showed -19 total yards, -5 rushing and -14 passing.

Whatever hopes New England had of making a comeback after halftime were dashed early in the third period. The Bears were penned in deep in their own territory, on the 4-yard line. Rather than playing it safe, McMahon called for a long pass to Willie Gault. The speedy Gault hauled in the pass for a 60-yard gain. McMahon finished the drive by diving over from the 1.

Despite totally dominating the Patriots, the Chicago Bear defense was not satisfied. The players were so confident that, rather than concern themselves only with stopping the offense, they were looking for ways to get some points themselves. Defensive back Reggie Phillips put the defense on the board by stepping in front of a pass intended for Patriot tight end Derrick Ramsey and returning it 28 yards for a touchdown.

New England trailed 37-3 in a game

so one-sided it had become painful to watch. The misery continued. New England wide receiver Stanley Morgan fumbled, and Wilber Marshall recovered for Chicago. With the game well in hand, Coach Ditka decided to liven it up with a little entertainment. The Refrigerator treated fans to his unique brand of ball-carrying, as he blasted through the smaller Patriots for a short touchdown run to increase Chicago's lead to 44-3.

New England finally salvaged a trace of respectability with a 76-yard drive. Grogan passed 8 yards to Irving Fryar for the score. The drive did little more than save New England the embarrassment of posting negative yardage for the game. Chicago capped the game with two more points from its defense. As an added indignity, it was seldom-used defensive tackle Henry Waechter who tackled Grogan in the end zone for the safety to make the final score 46-10.

Chicago's offensive statistics for the game were good, but not exceptional. Aided by a couple of long gainers, McMahon finished with 12 comple-tions in 20 attempts for 256 yards. Willie Gault grabbed four passes for 129 yards against some of the best cornerbacks in football. Matt Suhey, a blocker for most of his career, enjoyed one of his better games with 11 carries for 52 yards. Walter Payton, bearing the brunt of New England's defensive charge, gained 61 yards in 22 attempts.

The story of the game was the Bear defense. Tony Collins led the Patriot rushing attack with a total of 4 yards! Craig James, who had rushed for more than 100 yards in each of New England's last two play-off wins, was held to five carries for 1 yard. Chicago defenders sacked New England quarterbacks seven times, forced three fumbles that led to 17 points for the Bears, and scored 9 more points on their own. It was Richard Dent's sacks and hard hits that broke the game open for the Bears in the first quarter, and he was voted the game's MVP. Although Super Bowl history is filled with fine performances by top defensive units, no team has ever put forth a more terrifying display of power as the 1985 Chicago Bears did.

ard Marshall drags down Denver's Sammy Winder in Super Bowl XXI.

CHAPTER 5

New York Giants

Super Bowl XXI

In 1981 the woeful New York Giants needed help at every position except linebacker. Anchored by perennial All-Pro Harry Carson, the Giants' linebacking unit was one of the best in football. With the second selection in the entire draft, the Giants were certain to get instant improvement at any of their weak spots. So who did they select? Another linebacker!

To many observers it seemed like just another chapter in a history of bonehead moves by the Giants' management. Giants fans would never forget that the team had once wasted a first-round draft choice on an obscure kick returner named Rocky Thompson. Nor would they ever forgive the Giants for losing a game in the final seconds of the 1978 season when, instead of falling on the ball to run out the clock, they fumbled a handoff which was returned for a touchdown.

In time, however, the Giants' 1981 draft choice proved to be a good deci-sion. The linebacker they selected, Lawrence Taylor, so dominated the NFL that opposing coaches concentrated on ways to block him. It was Taylor who formed the foundation of the Giant team that earned long-suffering Giants fans their first championship in 30 years.

Like the Bears, the Giants were built on defense, with a powerful ground game and a solid quarterback gradually blending into the picture. New York was committed to the idea that defense is the cornerstone of a championship team. In the 1984 draft, the Giants chose yet another linebacker, Carl Banks, in the first round. Banks, Taylor, the veteran Carson, and Gary Reasons gave the Giants a mobile squad of huge destroyers, who were nearly 20 pounds heavier per player than the average NFL linebacking unit.

The three-man defensive line was made up of wily George Martin, a fixture at left end since 1975, huge right end

Leonard Marshall, and relentless scrapper Jim Burt at nose tackle. These three, along with the linebackers, formed such a solid barrier that opponents rarely were able to take advantage of a defensive backfield that was considered average.

On offense, the Giants had been grooming Phil Simms for the quarterback job since drafting him in the 1979 first round. Five-foot, seven-inch Joe Morris had been pegged as a workhorse running back since joining the team in 1982. New York's blocking, however, had been so consistently poor that Morris could find no room to run, and Simms seldom made it through half a season without a serious injury. As a result, New York staggered through a 3-12-1 season in 1983, Bill Parcells' first year as head coach.

In an effort to get instant help in the offensive line, the Giants turned to the United States Football League. The USFL had signed many college stars, who were now ready to make the jump to the NFL. In 1984 New York signed two of the rival league's best linemen, center Bart Oates and guard Chris Godfrey. Equally important, they added a bruising blocking back from the USFL, Maurice Carthon. This threesome helped give Simms the protection he needed to survive a whole season and paved the way for Joe Morris to emerge as a top runner. The Giants made the play-offs in 1984 with a 9-7

mark, and improved to 10-6 the following year.

One week into the 1986 season, the Giants appeared to be backsliding. Unhappy with his contract, Joe Morris had sat out all of training camp and joined the team only hours before the first game. The Giants had then lost the opener to division-rival Dallas, surrendering 31 points in the process. Then ace wide receiver Lionel Manuel was sidelined for most of the season with an injury. There seemed to be little hope that New York could challenge the awesome Chicago Bears for the top spot in the NFL.

But a change in fortunes, with players

Small running back Joe Morris was a big reason for the Giants' success in 1986.

staying relatively injury free the rest of the season, along with Parcells' unusual coaching style, vaulted New York to a divisional title. Although the Giants rarely thrashed any opponent, the team developed a habit of pulling out last-second victories. The players and coaches also developed a closeness that helped them to stay focused on their goal of a championship. Unlike most head coaches, Parcells liked to mix with his players. He kept the team loose by joking with them, gave them self-respect by talking to them, and kept them on their toes by yelling at them.

In piling up a 14-2 record, New York earned a reputation as a hard-hat, working person's team. Nine-year veteran Harry Carson punched in with his eighth All-Pro season. Lawrence Taylor earned his sixth straight All-Pro honor, his third NFL Defensive Player of the Year honor, and led the NFL with 20½ sacks. On offense, Phil Simms quietly directed the attack, but he rarely posted impressive numbers and finished the season as the NFL's 15th-rated passer. Joe Morris finished the season with 1,516 business-like yards rushing. Silent tight end Mark Bavaro won All-Pro honors with 66 catches for 1,001 yards and was known for his determined blocking.

New York's play-off showdown with the mighty Bears never took place. Although Chicago had also sported a 14-2 record, an injury to quarterback Jim McMahon decreased the team's effectiveness. The Bears were eliminated from the play-offs by Washington. The Giants, meanwhile, crushed a strong San Francisco 49er team, 49-3. In the NFC championship, the Giant defense took over to shut down the Redskins, 17-0.

Their play-off dominance established the Giants as the clear favorite in Super Bowl XXI. The Denver Broncos, on the other hand, had survived a photo finish to earn a spot in the title game. Trailing the Cleveland Browns by a touchdown with time running out, the Broncos had mounted an incredible 98-yard touchdown march to tie the game, then won it in overtime, 23-20. The Broncos were led by quarterback John Elway, who had been a spectacular and unpredictable scoring threat. The defense was still living off its reputation as one of football's finest, which it had gained in the late 1970s. Even though this undersized unit appeared to be wearing down, it still boasted stars such as All-Pro defender Karl Mecklenburg and sack-happy lineman Rulon Jones.

The two teams had met once earlier in the season. Elway had been the entire offensive show in the game, as he had rushed for 51 yards and passed for 336 more. New York, however, had escaped with a 19-16 win on a field goal with only six seconds remaining.

NFL officials hoped that Super Bowl XXI, played in balmy conditions at the Rose Bowl in Pasadena, California, on January 25, 1987, would offer a similarly close match. With Elway's skill at avoiding the pass rush, Denver might be able to exploit New York's vulnerable defensive backfield. Mecklenburg, Jones, and company were given a good chance to slow down Morris and the New York rushing attack.

The Giants, however, suspected that there was an element to the game that the experts were overlooking. In practice sessions, unheralded Phil Simms' passing was sharper than it had ever been. The Giants believed that if Denver was committed to stopping Morris, then Simms could surprise the Bronco pass defense.

Unlike most previous championship games, neither offense showed signs of Super Bowl jitters. With the Bronco defense zeroing in on Morris, New York repeatedly faked handoffs to Morris and had Simms pass the ball. The Giants ran nine play-action passes on first down in the first half, and Simms completed every one of them.

But while Simms was performing surgery on the Denver defense, John Elway was bombing the Giants. Working the deeper pass routes, Elway set up scores with a 54-yard completion to Vance Johnson and a 31-yard toss to Steve Watson. In the first quarter,

Elway and Simms completed every pass they attempted, a total of 13!

Leading 10-7 in the second quarter, the Broncos drove into scoring position for the third time. With a first down on the Giants' 1-yard line, Denver seemed almost certain to come away with another touchdown for a 10-point lead.

At that crucial stage, the New York linebackers took over. First, Lawrence Taylor bumped Elway out of bounds for a 1-yard loss on a rollout to the right. Denver then ran Gerald Willhite into the line, but Harry Carson was there to stop him for no gain. On third down, Denver pitched the ball to Sammy Winder, who had led all AFC running backs with 14 touchdowns during the season. Carl Banks broke through to tackle him 4 yards behind the line of scrimmage.

The Broncos were about to settle for three points, but Rich Karlis missed the short field goal. After that series of plays, Denver gave up trying to run against the NFL's top rushing defense. The Bronco offense called 24 pass plays in a row, one of which ended in disaster. Veteran George Martin corralled Elway in the end zone for a safety, closing the gap to 10-9.

Elway shrugged off the disappointment and again passed the Broncos into Giant territory. But Karlis, who had made 11 of 12 kicks from inside the 40-yard line during the season, missed

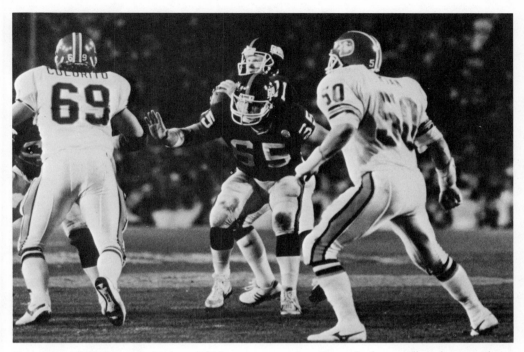

Quarterback Phil Simms looks downfield for an open receiver. Simms had an excellent day, completing all but three of his passes, to win the MVP award.

another short field goal just before half-time. Although Denver went into the locker room with a one-point lead, most observers believed the team was in deep trouble. Few teams could squander such scoring chances and still beat a team as talented as the Giants.

On the opening drive of the second half, Denver made what was to be its last stand. The Broncos stopped the Giants on third down near midfield. Instead of playing it safe with a punt, New York gambled on a sneak by reserve quarterback Jeff Rutledge. Rut-

ledge churned forward for the yardage, and Denver's chances of winning were as good as gone.

Simms connected on all 10 of his second-half passes as he led the Giants to scores on each of the team's first five possessions. Before long, the breaks were all going New York's way. The Giants even scored a touchdown when a pass ricocheted off tight end Mark Bavaro and wound up in the hands of wide receiver Phil McConkey.

The Giants' pass rush, meanwhile, had broken down the Bronco offensive

Carl Banks (58) and Jim Burt (64) were part of the New York defensive attack that stifled Denver's offense.

line. Under heavy pressure, Denver's passing game misfired throughout most of the second half, and the Broncos did not score again until the game was already decided. New York coasted to a 39-20 victory.

The Broncos had virtually stopped Joe Morris, who gained only 67 yards on 20 carries, far below his usual average. But in doing so, they had left the field wide open for Phil Simms. In a display of sharpshooting that may never be equaled in a championship contest, Simms completed 22 of 25 passes and easily walked away with the Most Valuable Player Award.

Coach Bill Parcells, meanwhile, walked away with soaked clothing, the result of a bit of horseplay that demonstrated the Giants' unusual camaraderie with the head coach. As they had throughout the play-offs, the players had celebrated their win by dousing Parcells with a bucket of Gatorade.